MICHAEL SMITH

Collected Poems

Shearsman Books
Exeter

First published in the United Kingdom by
Shearsman Books Ltd.,
58 Velwell Road,
Exeter EX4 4LD

www.shearsman.com

ISBN 978-1-84861-053-8
First Edition

The rear cover photograph of the author is by Barbara Smith.

Acknowledgements
The poems in this volume were previously collected in the following
volumes: *Selected Poems* (The Melmoth Press, Cork, 1985), *Lost Genealogies
& Other Poems* (New Writers' Press, Dublin, 1993), *Meditations On Metaphors*
(New Writers' Press, 1998) and *The Purpose of the Gift. Selected Poems*
(Shearsman Books & New Writers' Press, 2004).

I would like to take this opportunity to thank Trevor Joyce for his generous
assistance in helping me to edit many of the poems in this volume.

CONTENTS

Lost Genealogies & Other Poems (1993)

DEATH OF A BIRD-FANCIER

He fought death, it is true, to the very last
cursing the white coldness creeping up his legs.
His birds were still singing in his brain.

It was a note to be heard never yet heard,
a black tulip on the blue air—the unknowing
he lived among could give it no word.

And there—where flies in summer darken the air,
blackening the flypapers by the second,
in black gaslight and the pigs' smell and the poor's despair.

When the time came, I imagine the sun
set beyond the high grey wall,
beyond the innumerable railway lines and the Royal Canal,
and the birds at the foot of the bed were startled into song.

THE CHEST HOSPITAL

Long lane of black timber huts
desolate under high windy pines
where the wick burns to encroaching dark . . .

The orderlies deal with our chaos there,
efficiently,
with mop, bucket, syringe.

Flesh shrivels there, contracts, concentrates
to a final explosion of fluid,
the decrepit matter of the skull seeping away.

Before the end old men will not stay abed,
but try again and again to climb a non-existent stairway,
failing again and again

STREET SCENE

The butcher carried the cow's skinned head
by a bright grey hook in its eye:
blood trickled on the pavement.

The red-faced butcher felt
only the awkward weight
that pulled on the bright grey hook.

And there was the sun, too,
a hot afternoon sun; and children passing
who said to their mothers

'Mama, Mama, look at the moo cow.'
But their mothers dragged them by,
past the cow's skinned head and its hooked eye.

GENETRIX

The great snake with dragonhead
climbs upward, coil after terrible coil.

It climbs upward behind the naked woman
who stands, like some public monument,

in the dead centre of a single coil—
her hair is tawny as the great snake's scales.

Behind a timid waterfall the evening sky
is a deep blue pool, hoarding no stars.

Still, the moon is there— dull as a brown mud—
and a few clouds like small white worms.

Beside the snake and the wide-eyed woman
the prostrate sleeping man awaits his genetrix.

THE COLOUR OF GREY

Somewhere in Clare beyond fields and rutted laneways
two herons lifted into the grey air.

I climbed a promontory Norman keep.
Eyes swam over seas of grey rock;

And the dog at the head of the stair
trembled and whined in a grey fear.

The orchard was deadly sick with a grey fungus
and the bark of the hazel was silver grey.

The hair, skin, eyes, teeth of the old woman
who polished my shoes for the dance, were grey.

Here in October dawn breaks in sheets of grey glass.

LONG LANE

Long Lane, one of Dublin's back-streets,
just such a street as Mangan struggled down,
the winter darkness and the pitchy dampness . . .

Then, like some strange figure out of mythology—
a sphinx— the silhouette of this club-footed man
against the glaring yellow of the lamplight.

As the branch tip tapping on the window glass
in the snow-stormed night becomes the lost object,
to return always when a sense of loss occurs,

so fear comes now with twisting twisted legs,
hobbling down Long Lane a winter's night,
climbing steps, then knocking at a door, and passing in.

END OF VIGIL

Since now you're dead and I, I saw you dying
hours before that death
when life was flickering
delicately
like candle-cast shadows . . .

Through the window of your cubicle I saw
the first fall of snow
falling
falling
delicately
as only snow can fall

from long thin grey clouds like distant trains
travelling across the sky above the pine tops
their destination inscrutable as your silence . . .

as you lay upon your final winter bed
your face shrunken black upon the pillow . . .

Silence.
And then . . . *A stairway! A stairway!*
At the end of a corridor to nowhere
A stairway!

While the first snowflakes disappeared
into the black square of the chest hospital
A stairway! A stairway!

SWEENEY PEREGRINE

Because he'd lost his nerve,
  when they threw him out
he became a bird,
  growing beautiful feathers,
flying from hillock to hillock,
  feeding on delicious watercress
and, at night,
  perched high up in a tree,
dreaming of the wife
  he'd left behind.

Once, for some inexplicable reason,
  he was readmitted
to polite society,
  meaning human society,
but an old leering hag
  started him off again
with a ridiculous game of leap-frog;
  the feathers grew
and, airbound once more,
  there was no going back.

Finally, despairing of rehabilitation,
  he began to like being a bird,
to enjoy the watercress
  and the heady delights of flight
over summer landscapes.
  In winters of black frost,
with big brown wolves howling
  beneath the tree he's perched on,
he waits, in silence, for the dawn,
  with passionate, burning-red eyes.

FALL

The desolate rhythm of dying recurs,
the rhythm of outgoing tides, corrosion of stone,

fall of petal and soft rain on empty squares,
the fading memory of song, say, in an old man's head,

that never stops at a point of time,
a rainbow vertigo spinning beyond the nurse's cool hand,

subsidence of wind and branches against a settling sky,
and stars fading at dawn, or fall of snow:

Something ordered, yet desperate and violent—
A rose, say, or an old man's humiliation.

DOMICILE

Dead days, like a vegetable world all burnt up:
blossom and weed, rose and pimpernel, gone to the flame's mouth.

And there is no point in asking, no one can tell you why,
there is no reason for dying, it just happens that way.

In a cobbled lane of stinking pig and lesser celandine
a vagrant crone fumbles and stumbles among her pieces.

With querulous voice she hails to every passer-by she sees,
pointing to the green church dome among the hawthorn trees.

To every passer-by who will not mind her
The moon is a greener cheese, she says, *only kinder.*

The Gift

Through no imperial portals, but rusty bars on broken hinges,
to this kingdom of black earth like dampened dust

where my green knight evades the black-shawled witch's eye,
the dragon's teeth and the sly pervasive worm.

Bells beyond the kingdom toll the significant hour
and the streets are silent, the squares empty.

In his gaslit room of the golden birds
roosting quiet as the small rain of summer,

the old man receives the boy's green gift,
and the green knight hears his golden song in wonder.

Poet

There is something white and still in the black river
                below the cathedral—
in the black river quiet as the dark it flows through—

and no one can see it but the still man across the parapet.

Streets have fallen taking pieces of the sky with them;
summers have passed taking many who walked through them;
the spring is busy computing a new mortality list.

It has rained,
                it has snowed,
                                and even the sun shone
occasionally.

But the gaze of the still man across the parapet
is fixed on something white and still in the black river.

City I

Too soon put up for the wind that blew it down,
    hope became despair,
and despair was the sea on which my ship had sailed.

The rain became the city, the city became the rain,
and the unnested fledgling that ancient playful dog.

Barbara, Barbara, my canal-bank pinkeen girl,
your curls are in the water with the barge,

and I am sailing down a purple Nile
across the mill's aluminium-silver dome

from where the knacker's leans against the sky
and a solitary lilac weeps in its concrete yard.

City II

Here is the abattoir where, in the old days, were heard
the ultimate cries of table beasts.

Here is the home for unfortunate women
who launder a twelve-hour day and are never cleansed.

Here is the Union, picturesque on a sunny Sunday;
in fact, stables of appalling decrepitude.

Here are the slums where life swings back and forth
with a thud like a heavy pendulum.

Here is, partly, love's ecology: occasional blue skies
and, more often, thunderous falls of black stars.

City III

There is one, never seen, behind that window
where the light burns on through every night;

another, whose sole appearance in a generation
was a naked dance with obscene gestures.

There is a third, whose tired white face
forever droops from a backyard window

like some old flower that will not wilt
attended by an ancient spinster:

mad but quiet people, gone, like Elijah, up,
body and soul, into their own home-made heavens.

City IV

It was, the neighbours say, a considerable time ago,
but nobody knows the date or exactly what took place.

It was late summer, say, just for the neighbours' sake.
Imagine the afternoon, the flies maddened with heat,

the flies thick in the air, exploring every place,
and the afternoon there in a deadly prurient heat.

Even the old man's pigs lay prostrate in the square
though grunting occasionally at a black fist of flies.

It was late summer, say, near the seasonal change . . .
But nobody knows the date or exactly what took place.

Two Artists

The linnet on the orchard tree was green
so the day became an emerald, the branched moon a pearl.

Menacing gargoyles laughed below the turrets
but poet and etcher were two tired to hear.

And the world was tired of their excessive love,
unsympathetic now to all their fumbling gestures.

The stars were inedible, the clouds could not be caught,
the belovèd married another and moved away,

Arcadian lovers, dropt from the silver lining of their dreams,
their legs danced in a last impatience with the world's height.

ORACLE

Ghost, come and speak to me beyond the hawk's-beard,
the scum-surrounded yellow water lily;

tread gently the warm crushed brick of home,
and, upon the thistled hill of childhood,

speak to the assembled sunlit dust,
the heavenly host in all their summer heat.

Afterwards, in needless demonstration,
walk the canal water's hot and putrid surface.

I, like a dog's black skull in submarine sleep,
await your oracles from beyond the rubbish heap.

THE NIGHTMARE

Beneath the table the naked boards,
three feet of air above the black-earth kingdom
                              of the singing worms,
and the familiar trapdoor unbolts to the post-midnight,
the single shaft of sunlight through the curtains,
and the boom of the clock with the tiny pendulum.

Once more the gnomic face with huge fish-like eyes
glares through the opaque darkness.
Its breath is heavy upon the air like a living thing,
fouling the fevered night.
A moth flutters against the window and is still.

Quietly memory wheels to the past like a bird of prey.

Asleep in the City

Cold air glints
like frost against the stars,

and the moon's casual indifferent face
simply there
in the broken sky,
bird-high above
the small terraced houses
where people dream
in the hard night
of their own private suns:

red things beating still
beneath the packed snow.

.

Particulars

(as in a police report)

Here the walls breathe to the imagination's warm reception.

Shadows are everywhere, real and unreal.

Questions form in the darkness and remain there.

Glistening machines throb in antique skeletons.

A tree is an incongruity where bricks are growth.

The canal stagnates on others' putrefaction.

The convent bell is synchronic with the horse's last neigh.

Over the vendor's shoulder the hungry cry.

Poems for souls lost between hand and mouth.

THE RIGHT TIME

The time was truly right for the recall of stories.

The flesh withering to its own painful tune,
memory tightened its cords
for its last intense melodies;

love was crying out beyond the slow sad death:
the collapse of things like the sift of sand.

One Day

When he died it was still summer.

The street rose and responded
with its rehearsed platitudes,
innocently, knowing no other way
to remark his casual
but final disappearance.

The girls from the sewing factory
passed by at the end of the street,
singing as usual that Friday evening.

It was still summer, and like a heavy gauze
sunlight caught in the stench of the abattoir;
but no one remarked this unpleasantness.

His children played in the street that evening
and danced gaily on the pavements
to the frenzied buzz of the blue-bottle against the window panes.

MITCHING

Blonde hair at the edge of the pavement
caught in the sunlight like a bright leaf:
the dull classroom as far away as the heaven
of angels' wings that never crumple.

The lorries passing, the pigeons, the gulls;
smells from the factories, soap, chocolate, timber;
and the bandy drover's shouts that rise forever
over the thousand brindled backs of the cattle . . .

How infinitely important all that was
to the wide eyes under the blonde hair.

A big stick poised to beat their backs
when the drovers turned theirs . . .

What sense of importance swelled at the smack
of the stick on the dung-caked dumb flesh

LOST STREET

Always the old houses were falling into dust;
and the weeds grew high as the houses fell,
and gaps in their broken walls led to strange places.

Piles of red dust burned in the sunlight.
The slow, blue pigeons, the purple weeds.
A girl's soft laugh rounded the broken wall:
golden shards, old china, among the nettles.

Black, that city soil was black when you plucked
grass sods to drown the drumming on the tin roof
of the rain that always fell as the close of evening
as you listened quietly to the tense growth of sounds.

It was almost enough to have stayed there forever,
or at least till winter came and all was frozen.

Penny Dinner Queue

At the appointed hour they came,
from who knows where or who knew then;
from the farthest reaches of the city,
from park bench and slobland and river's edge;
from hostelries and distant places beyond time.

I can remember no details to speak of.
A queue of greasy men against the railings
moving to their own slow tempo
or the whiskered nun's brisk propriety.
I can recall the hour from the tolling of bells.

In the bushes the caterpillars are voraciously
at the sooty leaves.
The cakeman came with his trays of cakes
caught in their last act of decay,
dessert and industrial refuse.

I remember the summer as hot pavements.
The time is imprecise, but the place is there,
and the wailing of the factory sirens,
and the workers' clean sweep on foot or bicycle.
In the evening the air sank with the weight of darkness.

MURDER

It was the time of the big races
when prize pigeons, lost, walked into your hands.
We got up early and waited patiently,
watching the sky or, for diversion,
the sly cock's annoyance of the silly hens.

The afternoon stretched itself like a tired walker,
with the pigs and eternally old women in doorways.
My grandfather's room of singing birds,
canaries, finches, sang through the open window,
conjuring trees and streams to shut eyes.

At three in the afternoon,
in search of a cup of sugar or spoon of tea maybe,
a neighbour stumbled to a horrible difference.
She neither fainted nor screamed and,
by four, even the murderer was arrested.

It was the time of the big races ...
But something broke, anticipating
the blue hatchet's thrust to the skull.

Red blossoms of geranium
sprinkled the sunlit yard.

Dark Things

HE: These are dark things to speak of in a town like this—
not from any ponderous, sentimental guilt,
an imposed disposition to weep.
It is so because it was dark and night.

SHE: An inner and outer darkness of night
that would grow naturally in time to light
but could not be forced, not even slightly.
Something was burning through to put things right.

HE: As a child I danced my mad dance of sex.
I was, in turn and together, pimp, prostitute, lover,
belly dancer and passionate sodomite. I prayed,
both monk and frightened sinner in a darkened box.

SHE: Nothing was itself but the burning flesh
consumed what it touched in a dead heat of lust,
throwing not flames but dense shadows of smoke.
A limp couch was flesh I gladly lay upon.

HE: Dark things to speak of that linger yet,
follow me down these streets like sorrow's child.
Time that was surely more than I can guess
was quietly lost in a warm ingenious night.

MORGUE

The retired soldier spick-and-span in every detail
as his beautiful groomed silver moustache,
how appropriate this his last duty,
sentinel at the silent station of the city morgue.

No grieved relatives turn to him for compassion.
he is no more to them that the cream, aseptic walls,
the trestles or the green-veined marble slabs,
part of the scene to be confronted and forgotten.

To the not-to-stricken he will comment on the weather,
an inclement season's frequency of death,
the futility of debts incurred by funerals;
and then go to his lunch of chops and liver.

Once a body stirred, he recalls.
Bravely, he waited for further signs of life;
but the stirring stopped beneath the sheets.
Crossing himself, he closed the window
on the summer wind.

CHIMES AT THE CANCER HOSPITAL

Small things, like the turning of a key,
open, as light does a knot of petals,
the mind locked lost in a dead routine.

Things small enough
to have seeped through the pores,
the nerves, the blood,
into the brain,
till they are forgotten,
if ever remembered.

Such incredible foliage
outside the window.
The sun blazing
on its myriad greens.
And the woman sitting at the bed beside,
a stupid lump
on her neck,
big as a fist,
tensely counting the puffs
of her cigarette—
one— two— three—
and the white-blue
smoke fading
gently across
the glass partition.

Teatime. We go outside
into the sunlight
and wait. I remark
the lawn's green.
the empty pond
and the heat
falling in thick waves
from the brilliant sky.

A steeple-clock chimed.
Its leisured sounds lifted ponderously
like great birds,
rising beyond the height of trees,
above the bell-tower
and into the sky's blueness.

Love Poem I

Now the night prowls round my heart
like a hungry feline:
I cannot tell fear from loneliness.

The air thickens with ghosts familiar and strange.
Your father's footstep creaks the loose stairboard.
A picture suddenly tilts on the wall.

Our human losses of these past two years
have left their wrecks
whose bare ribs protrude in this low tide.

A prayer comes to my lips from childhood
but cannot be said:
our lost mariners are unreported yet.

Winter's Tale

The great white horse my father drove
hoofed up sparks at the closed door
till it opened and my mother broke
to sympathy with the dumb beast in the hard weather,
fed him more bread than we could well afford.

All that winter, every day, my father says,
the great horse pulled at the reins as he passed
our street. A beast easily harnessed to habit,
he had to be given a slack rein.
It was a bad winter and even the snow came.

Just after Christmas he slipped on the ice,
his great weight removed from the stability of earth.
His fall broke the two shafts, my father says.
His frantic breath clouded in the cold air
till the vet shot him dead there in the street.

The story goes . . . A great white horse,
a huge gentle creature, a mere dray nag,
slipped on the ice and broke his bones.
Time was then for the listening boy
the unmeasured heartbeat,
black hammers in the melting snow.

Suzie in the Magdalene Home

Who will speak now or ever for Suzie
whose confinement has stretched for ten years
and will doubtless stretch for longer
till her frail body,
wracked by a straying head,
breaks like the suds on the tub she bends over.

Suzie and the old woman of the Coombe
who bares her crotch to the startled respectable
and screams ruin on all exploiters of the cunt.
Suzie in her laundry convent tortured with salvation,
and the old woman in her back lane
chiding the crawling dark.

And their daughters,
products of aberration,
themselves aberrant,
lost in the city's asylums,
in their delicate heads
wandering an irregular cell's sly curvature.
Not even filed as missing persons,
it is as though they didn't exist,
hadn't happened,
like last year's pain.

Prayer

Tumultuous rainfall of birdsong
at this the door of another summer,
through a slow, insidious dawn,
steel-grey
like an indefinite sword.

Sleep, children,
out of harm's way,
till sunlight drives the ghosts
from the swaying air.

.

Moon Over Dark Buildings

Moon over dark buildings.
Warm nights of autumn.

On grass patches of wasteland
children's priapic games.

The boy with yellow skin
smooth as porcelain . . .
my refrain.

From the black sheets of sleep
the sweaty knobbly fingers of fear
plucked at me.

The house was in a deep sleep
as if it did not exist.

Moon over dark building,
warm nights of autumn.

Teacher & Pupils

The red squirrel
all co-ordination
lopes in perfect arcs
on the lawn's smooth green

Ears cocked
he peeps over
the garden wall
to observe
concrete
tarmacadam
pedestrians
cyclists
& motor cars

The brief intensity
of his gaze
is final

No place for him there

He returns promptly
effortlessly
to his green world
of grass and leaf

His bushy tail
arches in perfect symmetry
to the arc of his loop

From the windows
of our daily routines
declension/paradigm
we are impressed to silence
by the clarity of his choice

ACCIDENT

was it
by chance
the crack
of birds' wings
startled
the cat
so that
it darted
out
under
the milkman's cart
to be killed
at length
by horse hooves
and cartwheels
and the strokes
of a
scavenger's spade?
or a boy's
deliberate play
something to do
at the start
of an empty
summer's day
so that
he could
at length
say
he had experienced
an old woman's
sense
of loss
her whine
for a puss

gone
and never
come back?

CATS IN ACT

The wind howls
at the back door.

The nightcats
are softly afoot,
intent acrobats,
slipping down
dank walls,
gliding through
familiar crevices,
ranging their territories—
sniff sniff sniff—
exorcising
unseen intruders;
maintaining order
with arched back
and hiss.

Windows locked,
doors bolted,
the people sleep untouched
in warm beds.

Inside heads
a dark form weaves
through a labyrinth
of dreams.

A muffled cry
brushes
against the silence.

A daybreak
blood appears
to stain a white pillow.

DESCENT OF THE CAUTIOUS SPIDER

Suspended on invisible thread
the spider spins his way
down the lavatory's white wall

A small draught catches
and buffets him
like a storm

Displaced
his legs contract
and he swings
without panic
neatly
to and fro

Stationary once more
he spreads his legs
and spins again
towards the floor

Finally
no doubt in pursuit
of where he's going
he exits
into the night
under the door

PLEBEIAN

With a turn of mood
the cat is out of doors
comfortless

He seeks and gets
no explanation
accepts all
as inevitable

Momentarily
he stops
for the fact
of his expulsion
to register
with the vehemence
of the cold
on his coat

THE CITY IN SUMMER AGAIN

The children fill the street with voices
rehearsing the past play of faces
behind curtains,
cells of loneliness
where fear starts
sudden as violence.

Summer again,
sunless and windless.
In the soft grey calm,
convent and houses,
street and the trees
behind the towering wall
caught again in memory's maze.

It is a time for thinking of ghosts,
a quiet time redolent of sadness.
The past comes with a thousand voices
and the bricks and walls hold spectral faces.

Familiar footsteps on the pavement.
An ill-matched key fumbles at the lock.
And pity engulfs me like a chamber
for all the present lack.

HERMIT

He went into the mountains of Spain
      into the hoary sierras
      to find a clearer emptiness

He moved amid the people
      the good   the evil
      the open   the close
a mute grammarian

He listened lazily
      to the tinkle of the oxen-bells

He watched casually
      the men and women trudge to the fields
      and the children playing

All was
      as if he were not there

He closed his eyes
      was nowhere again

SAN MARTIN DEL PIMPOLLAR

Village of stone and dust

Sun
pouring a scalding liquid
through the darkgreen leaves
of the acacia
upon the hot stones of the corral
on the insatiable hens
and their magnificent cock . . .
and
on a spectacled bearded face
behind which
turning like the mechanism
of an old but well oiled clock
dreams of grey rain
a thousand dank steeples
and a multitude of tenebrous souls
familiar and alien
riding like gulls
on the back of a grey Dublin wind

Stopping to Take Notes

It is winter again
We are no nearer home
Outside, the wind lashes
the rocks and rusty gorse

★

Voices that know no intimacy
trouble the air
whispering of death
bleak company of crows

★

Home
Memory is a broken net
in a wild sea

★

We dream of spirits
Over the bare hills
they rise in their majesty
to eliminate differences

★

Before the high altar
we watch dumbly
the stained glass
gloss the vacant air

★

There is no solace
in the cold sea
the islands

★

The wind rises
The small black cows
huddle
against the granite walls

★

In the ceaseless pour of rain
the miserable earth
seeps a black ooze
into ditch and pool

★

The dead
make their exactions too
Someone we have not met
sent us on this journey

Connemara, Christmas, 1976

A Visit to the Village

No ancestral bones of ours
roll like ivory dice
in that black sea

No father of ours
drew his boat
across these barren fields
out under that sky
bulging with grey rain

We have no roots here
are not recorded
in parochial lore
of fairdays and fights
and reciprocated help

We are strangers here
come from the impersonal city
where rain hits concrete
with the shatter of glass

We have come here
to observe local rites
learn new words for things
and once again take not
of human sameness

Such roots as we have
we carry with us
in suitcases

Connemara, Christmas, 1976

GRANDMOTHER ABDULIA

The slow turn to death . . .

Inside the inner circle of grief
worlds fall apart

Grandmother Abdulia lies on her bed
saying nothing

Her pain flashes like fish
in the pools of her eyes

A personal history is crumbling
momentously
like a civilization

Winters and summers
in the cruel mountains

Births and deaths

Comings and goings

And the years of war

and the years of hunger

Images sear the mind
as if flesh

Reliquary

Voices   silence
Faces   darkness

Heard silence
Seen darkness

The beast's smell
in the silent air
clings
to the hair of the nostrils

Breath   not speech
in & out   in and out
foulness to foulness

The beast

We caress portraits
    tarnish mirrors

ACCIDENCE

The frail craft of reason
though seasoned against storms
shudders in the heave of pain
the wrack
                and is gone

With the knock of wreck
the friendly familiarity
of intelligible form
is instantly lost

*

Our poor metaphors
try again and again
knowing no better

With the abruptness
of accident
we are returned
to ancient
unparsable images

A pair of eyes
caught in a mesh of blood
adrift on the sea's surface

A Literary Life

Born in no year of grace
to ignorant folk
who abandoned him
without premeditation
to the street's
tentacular embrace;
its caresses filled him
with memories
he could never forget.

Years and years later
having learnt to read and write
he found himself in a story
fixed in form like a fable,
typed and coded
with scholarly inflexibility.

Since then
at every opportunity
he has pondered
the authorship
and circumstance
of his unlucky origination;
without successful issue
let it be said.

Meantime
the story unfolds.
The plot thickens, as they say.
Events combine,
work toward resolution;
the action quickens
or crawls along at snailpace.
Characters come and go

major and minor. Climax. Anti-climax.
A well constructed piece
of popular trash.

There is nothing left to him now
but to try to forget how it ends.
The only aspiration permitted him,
to enjoy whatever modest surprises
may occur through lapses of memory.

Love Poem II

It is not life that moves through me
but death

I watch the face of the sleeping woman
It is frail and sallow in the spring sunshine

This face I love
beautiful through love
is frail as the tissue of a spider's web

Dreams twitch its features
move momentarily like small clouds
across a familiar scene
altering mood   stirring memory

Unceasingly
death moves across the smooth broad brow
the tossed russet hair

Words on a page
Emblems of love and death
Deceiving order of sentiment

FROM THE CHINESE

It is not cosy to live
in an outpost
on the crumbling edge
of an empire
on the verge of collapse,
longing for old securities,
regular mail,
certain supplies,
immediate & effective
relief in emergencies.

The desire to escape the present
increases daily.
The world of one's childhood,
of one's youth and manhood,
is coming to an end.

All around
regrets are plentiful
and utterly useless.

My dreams are more real to me now
than these daily routines
of habitual survival.
And to think I was once a man of action,
considered myself so
and was so judged by others.

The Emperor's envoys
have been regularly apprised
of our appraisals.
Nothing, of course, is done.
Nothing can be done.

This is neither the time nor place
for writing poems.

Gamblers and prophets
are having a field day.

Hollywood Elegy

Light flashes off quartz
mounds of the past
burial chambers
passageways to death

★

Brick crumbling with age
mortar turned to dust
gaping fanlights
reeking corridors of the poor

★

Tombstone city
roll of tumbleweed
in the dry air
of the desert badlands

★

Birdsong in the branches
light touch of affection
word-stumble in memory
abrupt collapse of innocence

★

The leaves of the past
rustle in the skirts
of lovely women
angels of love and death
who anoint us with memory

Hide & Seek

High black railings
border the park

Outside and inside
are relatives

For instance
at fall of dark
all light outside
is glittering
various
voluptuous
vibrant

On the other hand
in daylight
it is almost compulsory
(one must qualify)
to sit on the sunlit grass
(always green)
and watch the familiar trees
(oak beech ash yew)
like a smug queen
in her caprice

One seems to know for certain
where one is . . . inside

Where inside and outside meet,
to make a presumption . . .

The points of the black railings
are sharp as split quartz

Whose putrid eyes
hang in the air
above the points of the railings?

From where do they gaze? At what?

THE STUDENT

Words were his special delight
and arcane knowledge

In his thoughts he had existence
as no where else

With studied melancholy
he walked the streets of his mind
not the concrete city

Birds in the ornithology texts
sang him melodies of unreal precision

Love was a game he played
with sundry sensory data

I saw him once kiss ugliness
with the passion of a philanderer

★

But the time of studies ended
that of endurance began

The pain of age
refused exclusion longer

Birds mumble now
on sites of dereliction

THE OLD MAN

Something snapped
couldn't be mended

The time of grief
preceded death
by many a year

Eyes lost their lights
Pace lapsed to shuffle
Things fell at touch
Anger was momentary
Love non-existent

The clock on the table
ticked against the silence

The glass of whiskey
was slowly emptied

Through fog of alcohol and tiredness
a thought struggled to emerge

Life is a thing cannot be reassembled
nerves crack that cannot be mended

FAMILIAR ANECDOTES

Odd to think now
that Father's familiar anecdotes
once impressed us more
than the rise and fall of empires,
all history's store.

Was it he knew the man,
witnessed the scene,
remained outside,
intervened,
named the streets,
recalled the precise day,
captured the casual way
memorable things occur?

The tales he told
bore the stamp of their chronicler:
selection of detail, snippet of dialogue,
joke, jibe, topical allusion,
all bespoke
the features of the raconteur.

Familiar anecdotes a father tells—
the poor man's chronicles—
veil the gaping mouth of oblivion
as any forest of family trees.

Suddenly I'm aware
it's my turn now
to make a fool or liar of myself
in the best family tradition.

THE GOATHERD

His clothes, brown loam,
his face, a tuber,
speech clogged with phlegm,
eructating at butterflies,
the half-witted *cabrero*,
despised by men,
descends the peaks of his anguish.

Abandoned as a child
to the goats of the sierra,
smelling of grass and thyme,
stinking of goat's milk
and cheap wine
he returns from the wilderness.

A beast like that has no soul,
they say;
he should stay with his goats
or go away.

No sooner said than done;
no sooner come than gone.

His visit at end,
provisioned once more,
the goatherd takes up his load,
abandons the company of men,
addresses the roadside poplars
and eructates at the passing butterflies.

Summer to Autumn

A child plays in the shade of a tree.
White blossoms fall to the grass.
A child's laughter lifts in the air,
a summer swing on the breath of autumn.

The old face at the street corner,
stupid with desolation, grief,
stares at the passing scenes of summer.

Patterns of sentiment cling to the air.
Vagrant memory stops momentarily
to stare at the laughing child.

And indoors, in the evening,
listening quietly, one can hear
the autumn lean
against the frail door of summer.

PLATONIST

The beast peers from the mirror.
Nothing's in order, it says.
In twitches of raw nerves
mind moves in its head.
With obvious pain and distress
it objects, it objects, it objects.
Life is not all it deserves.

Woman of flesh, it cries,
come and salve with your lies
the wounds of existence.
I never meant to be a platonist,
and now it's too late.

The disgruntled beast stares
at the horrid reflection it wears . . .
and objects and objects and objects.

NIGHT

Angels of darkness trouble the air
The beating of invisible wings
The broken cistern of flesh gurgles
Horror of dissolution
... am ... am ... am
Alba   light of dawn
Alma   soul of light
Human voices stir with the terror of rodents
... not i ... not i .... not i ...
Triadic incantation of appeasement

I run from my dream of night
The gashed lips of my wound are still

Voice speak   balm salve   lie deceive

Hog returns to trough
snout to float of swill

Visit

Night knocks unruly at the front door.

No, you are not welcome, stranger.

You require directions?

Well, this is a morgue
where the stiffs stay put.

There was a light in the window?

Of course there was a light.
Reassurance in these our vigils
that the dead are where and as put.

You wish to be admitted nonetheless?

Come back tomorrow when things are normal.

Dublin, 1980

THE DOOR'S TIMBERS ROT

The door's timbers rot.

Through hairline cracks
in their bland face of paint
the rain of rot has seeped.

Touch them with finger:
they yield to pressure,
collapse inwardly.

Through hairline cracks
the rain of rot has seeped.

What is essential rots.
What binds together rots.

The door's timbers rot
behind their bland skin of paint.

HISTORY LESSON

With what does the cry of men
form itself in the air?
With lung, with heart, with head?

Does the cry in the ancient texts
echo the struck beast
or the soul humiliated?

Cries of hunger, cries of fear,
cries of loneliness, the cries
of the doomed, ecstatic flesh.

The stone rolled down again.
Thistles grew in the corn.
Mortar perished, the masonry crumbled.

Icicles formed on the fingers.
The flesh singed and smelled.
Camps were pitched, moved on.

A child cried in the night . . .
Question and question and question
without answer.

The cries of the countless dead
insinuate themselves
across the millennia.

Meeting a Man with a Gun

Beware

No room here for argument.
All is certainty.
It is action that decides
and will decide the future

To straddle a fence
for a moment of speculation
with improved circumspection
produces merely an easy target
to be blown away at whim or by design.

Self-warning

Petit bourgeois indecision,
caution tempered with cowardice,
goes squawking to ground
in a mess of broken flesh and feather.

The main encounter

I faced the man with the gun
and asked him to think
speculatively,
to consider, honest to truth,
the multiplicity of situational factors.

He jabbed his gun in my ribs.
Petit bourgeois, you stink.

Bourgeois rhymes

Envenomed by poverty,
wounded in pride,
this agent of destruction
wears the beast's hide.

He dances unrythmically,
gun bruises breast;
he gropes clumsily,
he cannot caress.

Self-understanding

I know this man's hate,
the suppurating wound of injustice.
I know he hates the doctor
more than the wound.

Prole admonishes

When your weight breaks the back
of the tame beast that bears you,
in his place will come
a hungry lion to devour you.

Irish Report

1.
Cracking up and crumbling down
grey buildings of myth and death
as in the haunted mind of Piranesi
cast historic shadows

2.
Doors on a jar
windows of expectant fear

The bars of the curtain
stir in the sick room

Someone is looking
Someone is coming
Someone is passing

Wait awhile
Something must happen

3.
Predator leaves his kill
having imposed his will
leaving us to stare
at the martyred whore
of Charles Baudelaire

4.
No phoenix rises from the GPO
No where to go   No where to go

5.
It is our condition
always to look for something
beyond our daily bread
to dignify dying
and justify the dead..

6.
Something unspeakable hangs
in the dark mouth of the wardrobe

A shredded tongue

7.
Gallows and guns
Gallows and guns

Images of perdition
in the best Irish tradition

Verlaine's Pilgrims

In a time-worn park, withdrawn and icy,
a moment since, two shapes passed by.

Their eyes are dead, their lips unnerved,
scarcely audible their words.

In a time-worn park, withdrawn and icy,
two ghosts recalled the past awhile.

'Remember our ecstasy of long ago?'
'Why have me recollect that now?'

'Does your heart still beat to my name's mere sound?
Do you still see my soul in dream?' 'I don't.'

'Ah those beautiful days of unspeakable rapture
when we joined mouth with mouth!' 'Perhaps.'

'How blue the sky was, hope how splendid.'
'To a black sky, beaten, hope has fled.'

So they went walking through oaten grass
and night alone heard what they spoke.

PRECIOSA

Playing on her parchment moon
Preciosa sets the scene,
taking an amphibious path
of crystals and of laurel trees.

Fleeing from her rhythmic tapping
the starless silence now descends
where the sea resounds and beats
and sings its night-time full of fins.
On the summits of the mountains,
fast asleep, the frontier police,
guarding from harm the white towers
where the English people live.
And the gypsy folk are gathering
for their amusement from the brine
rounds bowers of triton shells
and branches of the greenest pine.

★

Playing on her parchment moon
Preciosa comes along;
on seeing her, the wind arises,
the wind that doesn't sleep at all.
Saint Christopher in all his nudeness
with his celestial tongue replete,
gazes at the young girl playing
a sweet and absent flageolet.

Allow me, child, to raise your dress
and see you as I wish to do.
Open to my ancient fingers
the blue rose of your womb.
Flinging aside her tambourine,

Preciosa runs in fright;
the virile wind takes up the chase,
pursues her with his burning knife.

The sea stills its murmuring voices;
the olive trees begin to pale.
The flutes are singing of the shade
and the smooth gong of the snow.

Run, Preciosa, run!
or the green wind will catch you.
Run, Preciosa, run!
Look at him, how he comes!
The satyr of setting stars
with his shining tongues.

★

Preciosa full of fear
gains entrance to a nearby house,
higher than the tallest pines,
which the English Consul owns.

Three frontier guards are on their way
frightened by the shouts they hear;
their black capes cling tight and close,
their caps are down about their ears.

To the gypsy girl the English gent
offers a glass of lukewarm milk;
he offers, too, a glass of gin
which Preciosa does not drink.

And while in tears she tells the tale
of her adventure to those folk,
the wind in its mad fury stomps
and rages on the tiled roofs.

NECKLACE

Beyond crumbling wall,
pocked, scabrous;
beyond yard of mauve thistle,
indeterminate scrub;
beyond cat-prowl, pigeon-coo;
through small-paned window;
in the mote-filled light;
against fungoid wall,
pocked, scabrous;
wavering distortion
of candleflame;
papersound of mice
in the staircase bunker;
diminutive avalanche of ember,
age in the air as skinflake;
shriek of memories
beyond eardrum . . .

Quiet, quiet . . .
To your places.

Desiccated wings and legs,
torsos, disembodied heads,
tremulous in the spiderframe.

Winnowing grey sough
through interstices of thread.

Pendent yard of death;
shadowy necklace
on the throat of the summer wind.

CATDREAM

Shaded by the blossoming elderberry
the black cat stretches voluptuously
on the coal bunker's cool surface.

Awakening from its feline somnolence
of blanket darkness and click of sound
it raises the disdaining head of a queen

to survey the garden's green,
the gentle movement of leaf and stem,
the bits of blue through tenting foliage.

Supple as liquid its fellows pass along wall-tops,
carefully treading territorial boundaries,
halting abruptly, stock-still,

to sniff inquisitively
with momentary intentness
before moving on in the ponderous sunshine.

A child cries beyond boundary wall.
Its mother soothes with coo and caress.

The afternoon composes itself, wilfully,
in the dream of a cat on a coal bunker.

In the Shadow of the Cathedral

In the shadow of the cathedral,
in the back lane off the high street,
on two acres of the city's oldest muck,
the dogs of want scavenge
amid excrement and the wormy legs of children.

Old rotten heart of the city,
by your scabrous walls,
I stroll with averted eyes,
pondering time's evil.

Overhead, the slate-blue sky;
below, the sluggish river;
and in this wicked heart of mine
a wound that will not heal.

Cock of steeple, clock of tower;
the wind carries away time's evil
beyond the points of the compass
and the interdiction of the chronometer.

Crooked lanes lead to the castle
where the scions of power
meditate in the complaisance of longevity,
untouched, untouched by the sonority of bells
wafting their fragrance on the grey air
in the direction of corpses.

STREET ELEGY

In the darkfilled city's architecture
this room is a cell.
Here the contemplative captive
ponders the urban night.

Someone is strolling a thoroughfare
intimate with the furniture of the street.
There is arrogance in his leisurely pace.

Someone huddles, afraid, confused,
wanting to run from the shapes of his fear.

Someone lies crumpled on a pavement,
bleeding invisibly into his overcoat.

Dejected pedestrians
wend their way indifferently homeward.

Raucous words of song on the air,
shatter of glass, clang of metal,
and thud of something unknown against the unknown.

Across the bridge the bright-lit pharmacy
offers the all-night service of the city morgue.

Time to Go

Time to go.

Now the street's alphabet
will stare back indecipherable.

Time to go.

Canal bridges, towpaths,
derelict squares, ancient vagrants.

Centenarian brick rests nervously
on the dust of perished mortar.

Time to go.

Somehow here we found
the necessary mystery,
the whisper of past voices
we heard also in the leaves of books.

Time to go.

How long we looked
for the house of the ghost
we longed to meet.

Time to go.

Students of the past
tread cautiously toward the future.

Time to go.

Mr Sunshine

With the first warm sunlight of spring
Mr Sunshine bares his chest to rebronze
after his long white winter in overcoats.

Resuming his fixed place at the park wall,
balding head tilted back, spectacled eyes closed,
he faces idolatrously the long-awaited sun.

Day after day, from now till the late autumn's
occasional sunbursts fizzle out
and the wet grey blanket of winter
covers the cathedral park and its furniture,

Mr Sunshine can be observed every day
by casual pedestrians like me,
taking the sunshine as monumental god,
or, less godlike and more human,
waiting anxiously on the movement of cloud.

Delinquent Love

Frost glints in the gloomy air of evening
that tumbles leviathan in ponderous waves,
suspended, prone, in the narrow valleys of houses
where lights glimmer in small curtained windows.

No human sounds penetrate the frozen stillness;
only the distant tinkle of convent bells
cuts through the air like migrant birds
heedless of all but the internal rhythms
of their predestined comings and goings.

Beneath a dull street lamp at a laneway corner
a shadowy figure moves in small circles,
the slow rotations of patient love's chronometer.
Leaves scurry in fits, micelike, across black cobbles.

A door opens casting orange light and shadows.
Sudden voices grate on the wall of silence. A door bangs,
and footsteps fade down the tunnel throat of the lane.

Time now for the ardours of love's furtive rendezvous;
time again to be lost in the warm folds of love
as in the arms of oblivion, as in the cradle of the womb.

Mr Peregrine's Sunday Stroll

Far away in Tortuga bay
the pirates looked to the king of France
for legitimacy and women.
The rest they had:
riches, food, a pleasant climate
and the thrills of adventure.
Something is always missing.

A sly thought wanders
the labyrinth of consciousness.
No where at home,
it has not even a precognition
of the characteristics of home.
It only knows that finding it
will be its own death.

Meanwhile I take my customary stroll
through the little streets of weeping brick
and tired half-lidded eyes of windows.
The street trees are wrecked again,
hardly seem bigger after years of growth.
Mr Solomon of the corner house has died.
Cats, always supple accommodators, proliferate,
and dogs decay in futile sycophancy.
In such a place as this
even the grass struggles with encroaching moss;
weeds bloom like orchids, caravels of the grey street.

In the moist air I raise a droll finger,
pointing skyward its wrinkled flesh:
no place this for a pioneering stroll.

TODAY

This is today
again
one more day
to assemble the pieces
we call
we must assemble
to a design
that makes
the next day
possible
again
you who gave birth
and eased death
with love
worn time
to shreds
know the beginning
and the end
persist
out of reason
in love

MORNING IN THE CITY

Sunlight paints white
the river's parapet,
rest like the whitest snow
on the morning pavements.

The city is stirring
around the sluggish river.
The parasol trees
are in blossom.

Urban Elegy

Canalbank trees
branch in heavy foliage
across the towpath
toward the water.

Down a tunnel
of light and shade
summer strollers,

ghosts of summer,
fade in the distance.

Rented Cart

Just such a cart,
this and no other,
upturned to stop
the children
running away
with it,
was mine for the day.

No donkey beast of burden
was harnessed to its shafts.

Mine the strength
that turned its wheels
of fortune
as the children turn them
now at play:

a miserable roulette
on Dublin's bumpy cobbles.

CHILDREN AT CARDS ON THE STREET

Mary and Patsy,
Joe, Peadar and Willie
hunker on the pavement,
playing for the future.

Willie has removed a shoe,
Mary has a card poised,
Peadar is bluffing,
Joe is observing, small,
at a calculated distance.
Patsy is arbitrating.

No starched bows
spring like daffodils
from the girl' unwashed hair.
No shirt collars
spring like white water
under the chins of the boys.

It is no game they play.
They are old
beyond their years.

Three of the children
have their feet in the gutter.
One is gambling, intently.
Willie is clutching his shoe.

Two Boys on a Fence

Beyond the fence
no greener hills
but something different.

Who knows
what lies there?
The fence is something
to keep us out.

A girl peeing in the grass;
her mother in the window
anguishing
over her drooping breasts;
a hen, a goat, a dog that bites
as well as barks.

Such things,
prohibitive.

Whatever we see
we are amused by,
so it is different.

The Bird Market

This is where the birds sang
Sunday mornings in summer.
Canary, redpoll, finch,
disconsolate
dyed sparrow.

But the birds have flown.

Now a circle of men
toss for lost plumage.

Coins fly in the air:
heads and tails
on a dandruffed comb.

DISCARDED MADONNAS

Discarded,
the broken madonnas
do not ornament
even the surrounding rubble.

Painted plaster of paris
dissolving gradually
in the back-alley yard:
one with head bowed in sadness,
another looking heavenward
without optimism,
the third severely decapitated,
her head resting on a ledge behind her.

Two of the three figures
have their hands joined in prayer;
the third, her hands across her chest.

Who put these figures there
with so much order?
Three figures, and two severed heads,
on the white-washed border.

Tenement

Sunlight lines the stairs
making a ladder of light
to the storied heights above.

Paint peels from doors.
The floor is bare.
The arched portal
is an entrance to where
no one who lives there
would care to speak about.

Flecks of light
at the head of the stair
are ghostly children
stock-still in fear
of the invisible figure
behind the open door
below the stair.

In this place of gloom,
no sound of play or of living
troubles the air.

THE COTTAGE

Stone on stone
behind the caked lime.
There is a roof over her head,
no more, no less.

The door is ajar, the curtain asquint.
The dog on the threshold is real.

Flowers, in place of smoke, bloom
from the white-washed chimney-pots
outside the door.

This is the house they left,
sons and daughters,
the lost genealogies.

Here she has always lived,
and will live on until the end.
These things will hold till then:
the caked lime, the door ajar,
the real dog on the threshold.

Don't cry now, you.
From the darkness
of this half-opened door
we all walked away.

North Wall Dredger Man

The face of Mr Moore
is not visible
in the belching smoke.

It is there nonetheless
as Mr Moore sits
behind the sticks of the crane,

sinking the gaping
mouth of the dredger's scoop
into the harbour's water.

      ★ ★ ★

When Mrs Moore died
after eight children,
Mr Moore took a lover;

and the street sank
its gaping maw
into the wound of his flesh.

SECONDHAND CLOTHES SHOP

The empty belted coats
wait here for souls
to reinhabit them.

Hanging on nails
they transform
day into night.

But sunlight strikes
the weathered frontage,
and the shop's threshold

is a segment of light.
A single black shoe
intrudes from darkness.

The old black mother,
sits, in silence,
on her chair
in the dark corner of things,
waiting to seize the children
who pass by unwarily.

She will insert their souls
into her old empty coats
and send them out again

into the ancient city by the river,
to move again in tired movements,
without remembrance.

Liffeyside Bookbarrow

Here I bought my first books
with scarce pennies.

Joe, the barrowman,
could not read:
he judged books by your looks:

the penny section for down-and-outs,
the threepenny section a halfway house,
the sixpenny and shilling sections
for the affluent literate.

One regular buyer
I came to know
bought his books by weight
to sell as pulp
when they'd accumulate.

Between Joe's Charybdis of illiteracy
and the pulper's Scylla
I had to navigate.

THE CITY UNDER SNOW

Snow bandages
the wounded city.

Two Nuns Pass by Some Children

Who are these figures,
black-robed from head to foot,
striding the pavement?

In awe and fear,
the children stare at them
remote, incomprehensible.

Their faces are barely visible.
What bodies are hidden
behind the black curtains of their robes?

Their mission is godly.
Souls to be saved
in the squalor of slums.

A light, small and bright,
flickers in their shrouded darkness,
sheltering from the fetid wind of poverty.

Orphanages, hospitals,
homes for fallen women,
are their destinations.

Their feet move
as on castors,
their figures like furniture.

PEEK-A-BOO AT THE BAR DOOR

Prising the door ajar
she peers into the darkness.
Someone she wants is in there
hiding from the world and from her.

She is saying nothing.
It is wiser to say nothing.

I am here, she is thinking.
Can't you see me?

It's cosy in there in the dark.
The men are drinking and talking.
The old women in black are whispering.

It's cold out here in the porch.

Slum Children at Hallowe'en

And so it was Hallowe'en.

From the mask in the window
a tongue lolls across the lip,
grotesquely down the chin;
eyes stare out, skyward,
beyond the low roofs
of terraced houses out of sight.

I am looking at the window,
into the window.

Outside the window
another mask
with beard, moustache
and popping eyes
hides the child's face:
the child is father to this monstrous face.

His brother wears his own mask
that gives nothing away
but a beaten sadness.
The rest speaks for itself:
no socks in the broken boots,
flittered coat that hangs
in decrepitude,
the homemade ragbag
around his neck
like a convict's tag.

No speculations buzz
behind the wounded eyes.
Fingers touch toy,

cold chills the toes,
the evening darkens.

In such heads as these
thoughts would explode,
I think,
like bombs in time.

Messenger Boy in the Hardware Store

The hand scarcely reaches to the counter.
While he waits,
holding the indecipherable
paper slip,
the mandated message,
he stares dumbly at the array of tools
beyond his ken, not ever for his use,
not for hands like his.

The tweed jacket's stained and torn;
its leathered elbows hint of school
where likely he was no success,
or else the jacket was not always his.

The way his body rests, limply,
against the counter
suggest defeat.
     Spent matches,
a piece of string, a scrap of paper
litter the floor at his feet.

Two Slum Brothers

What can it be at the alley's mouth
that arrests their attention?
Their mother is hardly calling them home
for their tea or detention.

One has a can in his hand,
though he is not begging.
The can with the hole, that he grips,
is for the dirt he is digging.

His brother stands soldierly at his side,
implacably staring.

At the alley's mouth
who knows what they are seeing?
Maybe the coalman has broken a leg
or a girl in the corner is peeing.

STREET SINGER

This is a song I sing
for my supper.
Rain down coppers on me
compassionately.

My voice is hoarse
but I know the words.
I have not eaten for days.
I frighten even the dogs.

Come to your windows
if only in curiosity.
Then rain down coppers on me
compassionately.

THE AGES OF WOMEN

Mother, enthroned on kitchen chair,
hands on lap, holding no sceptre
but a child's toy.
No tapestried background hers
but a walled doorway
hieroglyphed with graffiti.

She is alone among her children:
the seated one with patched eye
and arms folded like an ancient;
the sturdy one with ponderous bow;
the baby pushing her own pram;
the baby asleep in her pram.

In the darkness of the hallway
the silhouette of a sister queen
empties bucket to drain.
The domestic quotidian of their lives
is a muffled scream in the sunlight.

Imagine winter, my friend.

THE GOAT GOES TO TOWN

Billy-goat, Billy-goat,
where have you been?

In the streets of Dublin
such sights I have seen.

I've lived with a horse,
some pigs and some hens
in a back-alley stable
since God knows when.

But once, every Saturday,
I'm taken to town
on this two-wheeled cart
up hills and down.

The tall people stare,
and the children throw stones
when they hear the street-cry,
Any rags, Any bones!

WHEELWRIGHTS

The iron hoop
burns the timbers tight
in a geometry of hands.

They cannot read the stars
like the Incas.
Their wheels are not planetary,
sounding celestial music.

Bump of cobble and kerb
is their consideration:
winter slush and summer rain,
ice and smooth rotation.

SACRED HEART

Sacred heart of Jesus.

Arms extended to the world,
above the radiating heart.

Be at peace.
Take it easy.
You're going
nowhere
at whatever speed.

The hands perforated
so we know
that you know
what you're talking about.

One night
a small fluorescent
light danced
across your brow.
It was pitchblack,
moonless and starless.
There was no wind.
The curtains were pulled.

From my bed
I could hear
the cacophony
of drunken voices.

Testimony

On his way
to Mount Venus
George Moore
passed by this house
and remarked
its window canopy.

I forget
the details
of Moore's anecdote.

An amusing story,
no doubt,
larded with lies
and half-truths
in the author's
customary manner.

But the canopy
is still there
in Pleasants Street
as a testimony.

SUMMER SQUARE

I am back in the Square.
Empty clothes flap on the lines,
sad buntings,
make soft monuments.

Almost empty of people.
Only two shadowy figures:
a child framed by a door
and a despondent adult.

The pigs grunt
in the timbered sty
against the boundary wall.
The cock behind the fence
crows in the afternoon silence.

This is not the Spanish
siesta sunlight I know,
with shawled old women
hiding deep in their houses.

Sunlight falls here
as on tombstones.

Out On Grass

Stabled where
they may be stilled,
their carts stopped
where the thistle bolts.

Gone to grass and weed,
beyond this waste,
their chains shed
autumns of rust.

Cries of the summer
and winter street,
echoes of toiling
men and beasts.

THE AUCTIONEER'S BELLMAN ON THE RIVERBANK

He rests now, stony-faced,
observing the passing pedestrians.
Behind him, domestic hoards
for sale today:
mattresses, chests of drawers,
sticks of furniture,
lamps, mirrors.
                    He is waiting
for the minutes to pass
until the quarter.
Then, without rising,
he will sound the bell
and announce the sale in progress.

Pass through, pass through.
Straighten and dust the mirror.
Consider the empty bookcases.
Ponder the stopped pendulum.

There is time still.
Cold clapper strikes.
There is a sale in progress
on the riverbank.

TWO OLD LADIES KNITTING IN THE PARK

No Penelopes these,
awaiting a long-absent
dear-loved spouse;
epically
contending with
rival lovers.

O but they bide their time
like Penelope,
knitting their memories,
stitch by stitch,
as the leaves behind them
knit in foliage
into the summer's fabric.

Their summer is long gone.
Emptied wombs of the world,
never to be filled again.

HANGING SHOES

O Lord,
the feet that filled these shoes
strung
and hanging like garlics
from the timbered post,
have walked their last.

They are beyond repair.

Let us pray.

Child Clutching Doll

Child of the wars.

The anonymous firing-squad
has left
as is customary.
The masonry is pocked
by time and bullets.
Its handiwork remains.

Blood pools black
in the pavement crevices.

The door you lie against
is closed.

This doll, child, you clutch
to your breast
is no shield.
It is your self-suffering twin.

Fallen warrior
defeated before battle.

Your uncrested helmet
tents no golden curls
but crawling lice.

VIGIL

What have you not seen,
mother, pass in and out
through this door?

Life and death,
mother, customer
and whore.

What have you not seen,
mother, from that place
on the steps?

Life bawling,
mother, and death
and death and death.

Ragstore

Rags strung out,

withering,
fall, as on
a forest floor.

Or.

Flayed skins
of the living,
snake slough.

The haze of light
filtering from above
cannot reach
the rotting depths.

Old Woman Behind Broken Panes

What do you see now,
old mother?
What do you hear now,
old mother?

Children playing
below the flaking sill
could kill, could kill.

Woman Chopping Wood

The axe chops at the great beam.

Behind,
in sunlight,
the wreckage of the house.
Dense shadows in the alleyway
where life once thronged.

Behind the bent figure
a mongrel spotted dog
placidly observes
two sparring cats.

Curiously,
with saw and axe,
our woodcutter
bends to her chore.

Witch of the wood?
Mother of firelight?
Crone of dereliction?

The beam of the house is still standing
cruciform with the chimney breast.

Snug

                    Old women smoked,
and sipped their stout.

Not a child in the house washed,
and the streets well aired.

But there's no anger in the face
of the young girl at the door,
the court's ambassador.

Scholars and courtiers
of life's affairs,
they hatched strategies

in the enemy's lair,
cool, suave,
debonair.

Backs to the Camera

This is the man,
faceless,
right hand in trouser pocket,
hat, not cap, on head,
hair cut tight to the scalp,
legs together.

He refuses to sit
on the vacant stool beside him.
He prefers the vertical
posture.

All backs
face the camera,
enigmatically.

Was it summer?
Yes, it was summer.

Sunlight lies
like dust
on the moment.

Through the Dark Eyes of My Curtain

When I was ten or thereabout
I thought I'd surely die
at twenty one or so
and that would be
very old indeed and enough.

My fantastical birds,
pigeons and finches,
canaries, thrushes and blackbirds
would fly away regardless
like leaves on the wind.

BACK ALLEY

I must walk through this door.

Someone waits for me on the threshold,
beckons me with the presence of boots.

I'm coming, I'm coming, I'm coming.
Poor ghost,
what need have you for company?

What can I offer you?
Why do you call me?
What solace can I give you?

I understand.
I have said it before to no avail:
te absolvo, for want of a priest.

No gold lights the alley's mouth.
It is the Holy Ghost in despair.

City Child Digging a Hole

There is no gold here,
no Viking remains,
nothing precious here
in the ordinary sense,
where the boy has scooped
out a circular hollow
strewn with pebbles and shards . . .

Only himself.
With his pudgy fingers
he feels shape and texture.
He is thinking of nothing
in this hollow of time.

INTERIOR WITH CAT

The cat has ignored
the hand outstretched
across the mouth
of the doorway;
and now,
with feline calm,
he stops in the interior
square of sunlight.

This is a place
you should not be.

The unpeopled dark
is heavy with damp;
odours rise
from rotting boards
and ooze from walls
of putty-soft plaster.
Grass encroaches
on the threshold.

No diabolical cauldron
bubbles
under glowing coals.

No shrieks or screams
rend the blackness.

A slithery pit
awaits on the edge of things.

SUMMER ANGLER

Neither wind's buffet
nor spit of rain, but
only a tremor
of the web's thread,
agitated, irregular,
jerky as panic,
attracts his attention.

Without circus-grace,
sprightly then he moves
his hairy torso
on sprawling spindle-legs
across his mesh of death.

What sticks stays:
moth or fly or bee,
beetle or butterfly.
This cast-net fisher
of the summer air
plays no sporting line:
this patient predator
kills to dine.

ANIMANIKIN

She crouches
rabbit-like in the dark grass
eardrums tense
nostrils sniffing the wind

I will draw close
to the animal
where I was born
where I will die

Lights like St Elmo's
crackle white and blue
on the tips of her fur

What she needs to know
is borne on neural waves
flushing the grasses
say, wingbeat of bird

O
I am tired of this animal
I have grown to hate

her sounds and smells
I must articulate

VETERANS

Before age had done its work,
angina and the effects of gas
had brought him low, the old man
in the cottage corner, useless
as the cindered fire where he still sat.

Invader, hun and jerry,
Teutonic horde, horse and tank
and gun, medallioned honour,
little Belgium and blood-mudded earth . . .

Time at his back not beck,
memories falling like ashes
through the grid of his daily needs:
a coat to take him to the sea,
shoes that wouldn't pinch
or let in the wet, quiet,
a new set of dentures
to chew the cud of his days.

No retired, slippered general this,
poring over maps, pondering
miscalculations of tactics,
the making of history,
names of the renowned dead . . .

The rancorous old woman at his side
broods on the past.
She, too, was part of the great war.

OLD COUPLES

Old couples,
ghosts of their past lives,
speech now redundant,
strolling their familiar streets
in a ceremony of sadness.

A winter sun with spring heat
eases their stiff joints;
a gentle breeze
brightens embers of memory.

Hard to believe that once
their love was passion;
the other unthinkable,
both one, indivisible.

And even now along this ancient street,
past rusting railings and peeling paint,
a kind of love survives the harm of time.
And their two lives still hang together,
shreds of curtain against dirty panes.

Murder Poem

Hammer breaks the skull
blood spurts from grass hair
& hammer-head
imbeds

Disbelief

A rat noses its business
through the dark filth of the canal

A small black waterhen
with orange bill
dips

A wild duck with her new clutch
steers a centre course

MOLE DARKNESS

He moves warily
in his immediate world:
a little run of excitement,
a brief pause,
a furtive and frantic bolt,
a deathlike stillness.

Overhead
weeds and grass glint;
air
sunbright,
white birds
floating high above the trees:
a banned world.

In the mole darkness
through tunnels tight
with scent and touch,
rain is the trickle
of stalacticial drops
from the roots of trees.

MINE

Down the throat of the main shaft
I drop a stone and count
till ten before the crack of stone
on stone sounds in the night

Eerie in moonshadow
rags of lime-white
black beams awry
irregular rise and fall
of granite ways
dense with pungent basil

They worked and spoke
in stone the ghosts
of this abandoned mine

The when and how of it
are vague now in memory
but Father and Grandfather
once toiled there
under the hammer
of our Andalusian sun
and in the sierra's
winter vice

Before their natural time
they died of lung disease
Father and Grandfather

Others died below
buried alive
some never found

Summer and winter
twice a year I come
as others to a cemetery wall

Córdoba, Summer, 1988

PEPE THE CARPENTER

I Pepe the carpenter
the joiner
maker of superb furniture
am now a business man,
a hotelier in a small way

My story of modest success
is one of failure

My hands that deal with note and coin
ache for chisel and plane
hammer and saw

My nerves are bad as they say

Only drink makes me sleep

I distract myself with fantasies
of girls dogs and guns

My wife abides the unhappiness

My eldest sun knows I'm a failure
and he hates me as I hate him

Córdoba, Summer, 1988

YOUNG VILLAGE DRUNK

The anesthesia of drink
is now my necessity

The village knows it and I know it

Despite my bad leg
the family curse
I never fall down
in the streets or in bars

I admit my speech
is now a mumble

It was my need to be loved
by a girl
uncynically
that caused my present condition

I am still looking for this girl
with diminishing hope

I settle
meanwhile
for the old whores

Córdoba, Summer, 1988

SANS CRICKET

When the time came to return
I had to guess
the purpose of
this gift of friendship,
this crude ceramic jar,
unpainted, unglazed,
a hundred small holes
in its sides like black eyes,
and a wire-held door
the width of two fingers.

Where was I then?

In a village
in the mountains
beyond a white coast
of the Mediterranean
where the sea rolled
for mile after mile
from an horizon
only presumable
and the salt wind
scorched with sunlight.

It's a cage,
Chema said,
a place of captive song
like a canary's,
to bring the fields home
and the sunlit mountains
and the blue dragonflies,
the scent of basil and thyme,
and sometimes
even a globular moon

mounted on a rock
like a luminous pearl.

You will close your eyes
and listen.
But when the cricket dies,
as it must, I asked,
and its song is ended?

It is the way of poetry,
Chema said.

Adsubia, Alicante, Summer, 1990

Death Poem I: Kathleen

This person is dying.

Let me say it again:
this woman is dying . . .

She will soon be dead.

Let me say it again:
she will soon be dead.

Again: she will soon be dead,
buried and forgotten,

as if she never existed.

Let me say it again:
as if she never existed.

Again: she will soon be dead,
this woman,

as if she never existed.

DEATH POEM II: TOM

When she died,
finally,
after all that suffering,
after all that courage,
suddenly
he knew again
his greatest dread:
that he was, at last,
alone.

And he knew, too,
that he had died.

As if going to work,
ordinarily,
coat and cap on,
he went to the river
to dispose of the remaining corpse.

ABSENCE

I leave the cup
and it is empty;
the door opens
and it's a gust of wind;
the doorbell rings
and the actor speaks his lines;
the clock's arms collide
at twelve
and you're no home.

THE WORD & THE DEED

O but I couldn't, however lightly,
casually, kiss her ruckled cheek,
or stroke, with tenderness,
the worn, hard hand . . .
                    That
was not her language or her sign.
Words are cheap, was her put-down
to all attempts to put love into words.

Perhaps she had in mind the giant
Webster I had bought for sixpence.

She little knew the deed could
just as well deceive as any words,
for all her deeds had cost her
sweat and blood.

MONUMENT

Because we needed something now
on which you could be named—
a small space for a legible hand
to write a common name—

I made a simple cross out of
the pole that holds the white
clothes to the clear wind
and off the dirty wall.

Before I Lay Me Down

Now naturally I place
my hand in yours
before we turn to face
the dark wall of sleep:
Hansel and Gretel
at the dark wood's mouth,
certain of nothing
but the certainty of doubt.

FLOOD

Dry skeletons
with other domestic secrets
floated out of doorways.

Did it rain
for forty days
and forty nights?

Certainly, for once,
the river broke its banks
and invaded the city.

The neighbourhoods
of small houses
on the river banks
were the first to see
their streets become canals.

From upstairs windows
grey heads drooped
to see their lives awash.

Only the children
were happy.
Cats drowned
and stubborn dogs
learned to swim.

When the bridge collapsed
in a tangle of metal
blocking the river-mouth,
the children were delirious.

The port gulls screamed
above the clanking of machines
and the cars were parked
on the hills.

PLATONIST II

Caged songsters filling half
the small place. A living library.
All came to this: a note of perfection,
of flesh and blood, yet impalpable.
His whole life, after all, a dedication
to a life of song— canary's, finch's—
something natural. Song to the ear
yet paradigm, out of time,
but, absolutely, in tune.

Summer Wind

Mid-summer
and the heat pouring
in scalding liquid
from a blue cerebrum.

Easy to imagine
in this ancient place,
a la sombra de la gran dama,
the voices of the dead
howling for life.

Segovia, July, 1991

Entering Old Houses

The jungle of reverting furniture.

Down the long hallway
a light filters through
leaded panes of a door
that now scarcely opens
to a walled garden
where thistles thick as saplings
conceal the earth beneath
hiding bones and spoons
and the separated crockery
of generations.

Suddenly
there is a crack and flutter
of wings.
Pigeons burst to the sky
that spins in a vertigo of memories.

. . . And Don Luis Spoke of Transcendence

Like slow heavy birds
bells toll
across the Sunday morning

They are in time
and out of time

Winging
laden with memories

Mythic childbearing storks
to Spanish steeples

Black-back gulls
to the river-mouth

The intricate tracery
of their flight
teases the brain
with persistence

Bells and birds beating the air
nowhere beyond somewhere

COUPLE

I don't want to go, she said
crying, not looking.

His hand a claw
that gripped its prey
with a solid ferocity.

I can tell you no more.

But the sunlight of the afternoon
burned in a bonfire of misery.

Winter in the City

The street shivers in the grey dawn.
Ice clings like flesh to the window panes.
Familiar footsteps echo down the street.
Mother is up and gone to town.

Some time, not too far away, I thought,
there will be another dawn like this.
Traffic will rumble vaguely in the distance
and the ice still cling to the window panes.

I'll wait then, if I can, if I may,
until a little late sunshine loosens
the solid winter grip, and I can hear again
the clop of horse-hoofs and those familiar steps.

FAMILIAR TROLLS

Morning
not night.
People walked
the sunlit streets
as normal ghosts.
Mother had gone to town
and wouldn't be back
till angelus time.
Arms outstretched,
leaping hurdles,
the clock was in a
countdown to frenzy.
No boards creaked
in the concrete cell.

No where to go.
No one to call.
A drama of waiting.

The trapdoor where none is
under the bed
may
at any moment now
release the heads
of my familiar trolls.

DWELLING

Too squalid even for a stop-over,
this poor house set in the mouth of the valley.

The road to it rocky and painful
with thoughts of the return journey.

No lodge-keeper is thought worthwhile
for this dwelling in the mountains.

Even the fishing boat gets stuck on the frozen bank.
Scarce fire burns on the freezing level.

Outside, only flecks of white cloud.
A gibbon listens to the solitary night bell.

(*After* Wang Wei)

W.H. Hudson on the Pampas

I

The fear of death came back,
not as when a bird is shot
and drops dead vertically
like a stone . . .

But when a cow was slaughtered,
not, as sometimes,
out on the vast plain like a sea,
out of sight . . .
but driven hard by against the house
for mere convenience

II

A mounted man
tosses a lasso on its horns
and rides away at speed
to tauten up the rope.
Another man dismounts,
runs up behind the struggling beast
& with two knife-blows,
quick and deliberate,
severs the tendons
of its hind legs.

III

The animal haunched down,
the man flits
from side or front

& thrusts his knife's long blade
into the animal's throat

above the chest,
working it
round & round.

IV

Blood gushes
from the tortured beast,
bellowing now in pain,
still standing on its forelegs.
The man leaps
upon its back,
prodding his spurs
into its sides.
The flat of his knife as stick,
he jockeys the dying beast
like a demon rider.

The animal down,
the men run towards it
& throw themselves
on its quivering side
as on a couch,
making & lighting
their cigarettes.

V

The ombús
bulge in girth,
monstrously,
to forty
even fifty feet.
The only tree
native to the svelte pampas.

VI

A knife can cut
their soft & spongy wood
that will not burn;
it rots away
like ripe water melons.
Its leaves are large, deep-green,
glossy
& poisonous.

VI

The ombús mark a place
on the endless plains
as masts of ships a port;
give shade to cattle & sheep
in the scorching siesta;
they act, too, as violent remedy
for the native herbalists.

VII

In one of these we built
our house of childhood play
for high noons
when the adults were asleep.

Among the twenty five ombú trees
there grew,
         I don't know
why or how,
a tree with no name.

VII

It grew , solitary, beside the house.
The only tree of its kind
in the entire world—-
sui generis—- many said.
Old & large,
its bark leprous white,
its leaves long
         smooth
            undeciduous.
It blossomed in November—
midsummer on the pampas.
Its tiny flowers
little tassels of wax,
of pale-straw colour.

VIII

The soft winds of summer
spread its fragrance,
when it flowered,
for miles around.

Then the neighbours came
to pluck a branch
& set it up at home:
the joss-stick of the pampas.

Matter of Seeing

I came into the world

I saw it
I cannot forget

it

From nowhere to somewhere
I saw it

Was it there
before I saw it
I saw it

When I saw it
it was there

I cannot forget
that I saw it
did see it
saw it
it was seen

but I saw it   it
I saw it

I

THE CAGE

There is a plastic rose in the cage.

The floor of the cage opens
like a trapdoor.
I remove the plastic rose.

That's fine,
Eppie says.

But the empty cage
now needs something.
It is incomplete,
purposeless.

Spectacled Teddy
not only will not do
but doesn't fit.

No, no, no, no!
It's quite clear
what Eppie means.

Still, an empty cage
is just as clearly incomplete.

I try again.

A tiny doll, a tiny seal,
Mr Frog, Mr Cricket?

No, no, no, no!

Put it away.
It's bold, it's bold, it's bold!

I replace the plastic rose
in its dusty cage.

That's fine, Eppie says.

THE PARK REVISITED

Chance or autumn
or where I am now
on this particular journey,
this time, this day.

Chestnuts, glossy russet,
lie scattered in the gashed
openings of their spiky shells:
unwanted pearls.
I stoop
and pick one up.

Paths long forgotten
bifurcate.
Each step flushes memories
from bordering herbage,
startles the silence of the woods.
The same small bridges
arch the same trickling stream
that drains the park
into the nearby sea.

★   ★   ★

Bright summer gone,
the sodden earth is heavy
and dense,
slumbering into winter.

Move on. Move on.

But it's no longer there:
the bamboo grove
I entered forty years ago

to arm myself with arrow and bow
against the dangerous streets.

★   ★   ★

The road roars
with traffic homeward bound.
I leave behind,
as I was sure to do,
my tropic jungle by the sea
where pirate ships ride
the shallow waters of the bay
cerulean as the sky
above their jolly-roger masts.

CLIMBING A STAIRCASE

Acknowledging the rites
of birth and death
wanted or unwanted
as the case may be,
loving or hating,
growing too old to care
or foolishly passionate
to the bitter end.
I pause, a hesitant foot
upon the stair,
unwilling to ascend,
afraid to go back down,
eyeing the half-opened
door where the landing
beckons in its nebulous
gloom, a pram
against the wall,
a bicycle without wheels
rusting on the boards,
a geranium's musty
smell upon the air
mingling with an antiseptic
odour and the stale
sweat of sick sheets.

I urge myself to climb,
supported by such props,
ignoring the jeering
cackle down below.

There is a window
that I know is there,
struck by sunlight

without apology,
cleaving shreds of curtain
hanging god-knows-why . . .

DEPARTURE

The valley slopes to turnips,
cows and sheep,

a small stone bridge
that humps a tree-fringed river.

Winter's grip
is not yet flexed to vice.

The air is balmy
in this early winter sunlight.

Change, though, is imminent.
Clouds slowly mass against the blue.

Always there is separation, departure.
The last of the blackberries wither in farewell.

(*After* Tu Fu)   *Cork, 1994*

William Beckford in the Escorial

In the Escorial, William Beckford,
privileged as usual,
saw an angel's feather,
casketed in gold and silk,
longer and whiter than any bird's
Beckford had ever seen.

It had fallen from a cloud
and floated down
gracefully
to earth,
undamaged and untarnished,
the stern-faced monk informed
Beckford not a little amused.

The turrets of Fonthill
never reached the clouds
towards which they climbed
at fabulous expense,
but fell, again and again,
block by block,
into a sad rubble.
Vathek was not amused.

Easier for an angel's feather
to fall on the plains of Castile
than for an English mausoleum
to breach the vault of heaven.

Winter Notes

The small-paned window
frames the silver birch
I planted six or seven years ago.

The filigree of its unleafed
branches sways against the blue.
Delicate delicate delicate.

And the blackbirds have returned
despite last summer's losses of their young
to pluck the red berries now in short supply

and stab at any worm in the sodden clay
while the cunning cat in the corner
waits his turn.

We are visitants only
                    the lot of us,
changeable as this northern island weather.

Birch   bird   cunning cat
and this gaze of mine
through the small-paned window.

Dec. 24, 1994

White Water

when the thieving
sea flashes white water it
will fit
in three quart jugs of the mind
sea of unending theft
flashes off the eyes
and roars
irregularly
in the human voice
flashes off the mind
and roars
for admission
to the human voice
touches chords
that roar
in silence
in the mind
touching cells
and land
beyond the white water
breaking on the land's tongue
extending
into the ocean
and the mind
blank
to be filled with the roar
of the white water
breaking
on the land
and the mind

listening

listening

TIME TIME TIME

Its dial's hand broken
the face of the clock still stares
up at the sky
in silence

I have built walls
symmetrical
boundary walls
more for myself
than neighbours

Thistles sprout
ivy
common ivy
covers all
sheltering
teeming woodlice
devouring all
in the moist
& in the dark

Crow's feet
hairs in nostrils
in ears
the skin pocked & marled
the mouth an empty pot
eyes dim
glaucous

THE DOOR

Closed
locked
open
ajar
we enter
we exit
anticipate
regret
encounter
leave behind
push against
slam shut

Discerning the threshold
we consider most important
Not seeing
we must infer the door

Then to decide
answer the knock
pretend we are not home

We are fearful
to leave and not return

FIRE

And the fire that burns
all uncleanness away
black bones to earth

The same fire
a glow of orange gold
alighting on a head
without ignition
or the eyes' flash
intolerant of touch

It flames
it flickers
seems gone
until a slight breeze
whips the embers
to billow and roar again

The fire denied
the blood is almost frozen
and the skeleton creaks
an antique machine
its purpose unknown

TIME DOES NOT ROAR

Time does not roar through torrents
or tumbling tides
or the beat of gong
or clack of pendulum
of a great grandfather clock
in an old country house
wainscoted
its leaded panes
catching the movement of light

but whispers through stones
and the wheeling of celestial bodies
where angels speak in numbers

or with the sound of skin flaking
from the living flesh

or the cellular relay that passes on
the message in silence

in silence

EILEEN

Not white for virginity
but blue
white breath
blue
in the heavens

You lay
clothed
in your habit of blue
in your death dress
blue
in your death box
blue not white

And white clouds
move across the blue
our thoughts
as they move
close to you

The blue dome
of the firmament
bells against our ears
space
remembrance
of ghosts

White ghosts
in a blue space

On the Edge

Posturing before death
the matador
half wills the bull
to rip a golden thread
for red flecks to appear
on the rich brocade
of his mortality

He is half afraid
until the moment
death comes
in a charge of rage

Autumn 1994

A cold wind blows close the door of autumn.
Its sharp brightness beyond a summer wind.

Leaves green as any leaves of summer
lie limp on air in resolute melancholy.

The terrible voice of the unstoppable accountant
ceases all labour, shocks the factory floor.

Somewhere there's a village sloping to a sea
of bobbing bright-green apples, flashing knives.

There, every afternoon, as evening falls,
the fishermen, replete with food and drink,

peer casually through the tavern's leaded panes
at the leaping sea left for the leaping flames.

The wind grumbles in the mast of the chimney-stack.
The ported sailors are content to wait.

Let the cotton fleet meanwhile sail above their heads,
bearing to distant cemeteries the last season's dead.

BRIGHTNESS

Brightness falls from the air
Brightness falls from the hair

The bright stick trapped
in the canal-bank reeds

The bright wind
boisterous in the bright air

Gile na gile
brightness of brightness
in a country's gloom

And Honor Bright

And San Juan's brightness
in his dark night

Brightness more than sunlight
more than moonlight on water

Brightness beyond starlight
beyond flash of bright eye

It may be no more
than the flickering
of a solitary candle

Nimbus   Halo   Aura   Karma

Eyes need never open
not even the curtain of eyelashes

Light floods the mind

Córdoba, 2-7-'95

The Red Squirrel

Twenty years or more,
through his generations,
a single red squirrel
went his daily rounds
in little leaps and bounds
and rapid runs
and prick-eared pauses.

We'd stop to look at him,
leave aside affairs of grammar—
declension and paradigm—
preferring the living syntax
we could see outside:
the short runs across the lawn,
the blink-eyed disappearances
into the dark shrubbery,
the daring marathon
of the long boundary wall.

Comma and colon,
exclamation and question mark,
clause principal and subordinate,
style abrupt and convoluted,
dancing diction.

Master of the green world
he circled daily again and again,
untroubled by the confusion
of honking traffic,
unstartled by straying pedestrian,
confident enough
to peer momentarily
through classroom windows.

He won the admiration of all,
safe even from the careless
savagery of schoolboys.

ELEMENT OF FIRE

You stand before the fire.

Whoosh, you say,
in a declamatory sort of way,
raising your arms
in imitation of the
leaping flames.

You know that such
flames,
flowering
up the chimney,
can burn
you
and cities
to cinders.

This was your
earliest lesson
in elements.

THE NICE DRAGON, ETC.

To the red dragon
belching balls of fire
you raise your gentle hand.
Nice, that's nice, you say,
in your habitual jellybaby way,
placating what is frightful
you think will make it go away.

You spot even the tiny witch
lurking in the corner of the page,
grinning toothlessly
as all witches must,
high-hatted and hairy warted.
Nice lady, you say,
thinking that will make her go away
with lion and tiger and cheetah
and all such beasts of prey.

You would turn
the jungle's rank undergrowth
into a smooth green sward
of delicious fragrance
with a gentle nice word,
silence the barking dogs
and make them sing instead
lullabies to happy neighbours,
turn magpies into thrushes,
sparrows into lemon-yellow canaries
to serenade all furtive backyard lovers.

And there was a man once
who stood on a hill in a faraway place
and spoke such magic words
to friends and strangers alike

who had gathered in a vast concourse
in expectation of something more difficult.
Out of his mouth words flew through the air
alighting like gentle birds
on callused shoulders
and grimy matted hair,
and they sang like nightingales
the sweetest songs ever heard.

Witch or warlock
lurking in page corners,
hissing cat or snarling dog,
all fearsome things we live among,
won't go away at the gentle word.
No matter.
Gentleness has such power
even Prospero laid aside
his wand of wrath
for the soft sway of words.

WHERE HAS JOE GONE?

Where has Joe gone?
They carried him out of the house
in a plastic deathbag
and they were wearing gloves.

Joe's window is closed now
so the cats of night are lonely.
Joe won't cause any more trouble now,
make any more scenes in the street.

Joe's razor won't slit that bag.
He's in it for good now.
Joe's mother is still grieving
despite all the trouble he caused.

He could have gone sooner
but what did time matter to Joe?
He tried it often enough
but he always bungled it.

Joe's gone from the street,
gone with all his troubles.
The neighbours barely remember
that Joe once lived here.

It's been three years since Joe died
and it seems like a lifetime.
Joe's gone to eternity
where everything always goes.

No use lamenting,
it's all over & done with.
Joe's mother has cancer
and that'll be the end of it.

FOR ALICE AT SEVENTEEN

Remember.
        The same things
as with a single pair of eyes:
the old lady with her dog's face,
a door askew, a pig abattoir
where the pigs, under the electric
prod, screamed like children
struck.

        A hard city let me say,
but no harder than those fortresses
of Castile we've known.
The human foot leaves no mark
on its concrete slabs.

But we have watched, intrigued,
the amazing patterns of water
swirling over its bed of stone.

Such things we hold in mind,
the stuff of flesh and bone.

ROBIN

This cheeky robin
who'll almost take
food from your fingers

who dares
the stalking cat
and the door's sill

who looks you
straight in the eye
inviting you closer still

Chirst's blood
on his breast
or a courtesan's rouge

trim as a golf ball
matchstick legs
quick as flame

is *your* garden robin
only in space and time
in *your* garden *now*

In all sense else
he's the cheeky robin
all others see

on *their* window ledge
in *their* garden
or on *their* tree

How curious to be
yourself solely
in space and time

and how free

Oct. 14, 1995

Antonio Machado in Segovia

I had thought, before this, of romance,
of adventure; Yeats in his tower beside
a babbling stream; stairs to the stars;
intriguing ladies in love with words;

the poet precious in his uniqueness;
candle and fragrant blossom, lemon
and orange scent on the moonlit air;
such things as these, poetical and rare.

But this was the room of a travelling rep;
bed, locker, chest-of-drawers, wardrobe,
a chipped chamber-pot under the bed;

a common room where common humanity
sat down, under the landlady's strict control,
to eat at supper the common bread.

Oct. 13, '95

LONG JOHN

Under the balcony, in the dry brown earth,
he hid the stolen coins while I looked on.
In no treasure chest or even paper bag,
the coins mingled with the earth that added
mystery to their metallic clink. A solemn oath,
fearful with threat, devised by him, bound
the pact.

       The air was dense with menace.

Was it days or weeks later he left me
alone, a five-year old, deep below
the riverbank, while the level
of the tidal-river rose inch by inch?
Briefly he looked down from the parapet,
his face contorted with glee.

He answered nothing to my desperate plea.

Down the years of his crimes since then
that I have merely read or heard about,
his devilish face has often come again
to grin at my childish helplessness,
recalling stolen coins, my abandonment,
and, most of all, my silence then.

THE GARDEN 1

The human face is a garden
to which botanical
principles do not apply
with any effect

Neither pesticides
nor fertilizers
ultimately
have any effect

The garden grows to decay

Crow's feet
hairs in nostrils
in ears
the skin pocked & marled
the mouth an empty pot
eyes dim
glaucous

The Garden 2

The garden once was
NOT
beautiful

But there was an idea of order

There was a garden planned
however foolishly.

THE GARDEN 3

The garden
always returns
to what it was meant to be
not by design
not mine at least
but chance

Who is the gardener?
Assiduous or negligent?
Weeds.

The tall rosemary died
parched
in the shade
under the umbrella
of the silver birch

Such things
plantings
herbs & flowers
of delight
to no avail

This face
will grow
into what the seed
determined
& the elements
chance

Sporadic attentions
momentous
—it would seem at least—
decisions
are of no avail

Loss of Currency

i.m. Ivan Turgenev

to have found such a man
inheritance dispersed
yet not quite

silence

still lingered
sudden hurt at a sight
at a sound
for example
the swish of taffeta
badinage
easy laughter
long ago

they say

a woman
broke his heart
impoverished his accounts
sold off his properties
a very long time ago

they say

tough men danced to his tune
a man of command
spoke French like a native
mingled at ease
in the very best circles
understood markets
and returns

voiced informed views
on home and foreign policies

reduced
they say
to remote charity
sufficiency
to keep a roof
over his head
a flicker in the grate
sustenance
to quell the rumbles
in his old bag of guts
closer

a cool breath arose

from the wide pond
that in the dark blue
flooded with gold,
above the tree tops,
the stagnant air
hung

water spiders gleamed
tiny bright buttons
so take it that
two loaches
and an eel
were the day's catch

the old man
stared
across the trembling
reaches

WORDS

by the birthbed
by the sickbed
by the deathbed

words

tearing
at the silence

sick
with the silence

sick
with the birth of words

words

are cheap
my mother said
little knowing

words

tear as talons
on dumbness

tear as talons
on time

against the years

no more than we
batter at doors
ramrod the silence

by the birthbed
by the sickbed
by the deathbed

TRINITY OF SORROWS

mater lachrymarum
lady of tears
standing in Rama
lamenting
her lost children

mater suspiriorum
lady of sighs
weeper of lost causes
mother of lunacies

mater tenebrarum
lady of darkness
singer of suicides

Graces Parcae Furies
our trinity of sorrows

Broken Dreams

from the Irish (c. 18th Century)

You passed this way last night, neither
too late nor soon; and yet neither moon
nor certain welcome held you back.
Spells breaks, I know, and we abstract.

abstract: to draw from,
to separate; as an action
from evil effects

But why, even for old time's sake,
not even ask for her who even now,
though she were down and fevered, crazed in mind,
would find your cold kiss warm comfort.

fever: a diseased state of the system

It is long days since I have slept,
not believing the kiss would never come;
and I have wept from grieving snow on sod,
knowing the sun and moon, and torch of God.

snow on sod: white snow & black earth

And though you promised silk and satin,
hats, clothes and fancy shoes,
yet I must still be musing: a bush in a gap
while the wind blows the washing dry.

Huckster

Minder of the till
until . . .
don't ask

It's habit . . .
the way
I've always lived . . .

with the till
until . . ..
don't ask

Texts for Irene

1

It is what comes first to mind
no more no less

The skull so fragile
it had to be surrounded
with cotton wool

Not even a duckdown pillow would do

The cot was a wooden eggbox
small enough to restrain movement
small enough to be filled
with the cotton wool padding

Such delicacy there
from the beginning
any human presence was a weight

Even the intake of breath
was an effort
as if ingesting a solid

But the cry was not weak
it was strong and persistent
as if it came from somewhere before
from something before
that knew itself

And it was not the cry of hunger
for the appetite was that of a sparrow
but some discomfort in the body

It was colic they said
wind astray in the innards
The weight of the outside world
was to be avoided for a long time
until the body adjusted to its new place
and could fight hostile microbes

The hatching inside the eggbox
continued for a long time

. . . to be told and retold long into the future

2

It was village without the usual topography

such as

a cluster of dwellings in a dale say
a church steeple
a humpback bridge fording a stream
a flooded quarry for summer swims
orchards to pillage in autumn
well known genealogies

Such things

This village was a street in the centre of the city
two short facing rows of little houses
ending at the high wall of the convent
the nuns' own village of chapel and school

of gardens and gravel paths
and tall trees over which nightingales sometimes sang

Mrs Doyle in No. 1 was a battered wife
Mr Doyle was an alcoholic
Mrs Macken in No. 4 had married very late
and had four children by caesarean section
Mr O'Brien in No. 7 was tubercular
and played the piano twice a week in a local pub
Mrs O'Brien was a virago who hated all men
except for her three sons
Mr and Mrs Love in No. 10 had no children
Mrs Love went raving mad at sixty
and was sometimes out in the street stark naked
In the back room of No. 12 there was Joe Halpen
whom no one had seen for ten years
though he was sometimes heard crooning in the early hours
The Scotts lived in No. 13
Mrs Scott had left after a row
taking with her three healthy children
leaving Mr Scott with the two impaired
Mr Brown lived alone in No. 18
His wife was in a mental asylum
and never visited by Mr Brown
The Jacksons in No. 21 suffered from genetic defects
which they kept to themselves
Donal Murphy in No. 16 played the violin
The Murphys were artistic
Ruby Jool in No. 17 was fat and cranky

In summer when it was sunny
villagers sat on their doorsteps and talked

Winter was ghosts
footsteps on pavements
convent bell in the chill air
moonlight on the slates
starlight above the tall trees

There is more to come in due time

3

A child is lost in the streets of the city

Memories struggle
with closed doors and railed gardens
hedges and weedy plots and dying flowers
and cats on sills of shuttered windows

A dog barks at a shut gate

A laneway ends in a blank wall

Old stooped women find their way
by familiar cracks in pavements
to the church at the junction
where their lord awaits
with a balm for their miseries

These streets are rotten with time

The child cries quietly and goes on
being lost
wandering and looking

for what will never be found
a home
lost

4

In the beginning
something stirred into life

It is not known why
though
            maybe
                        how

It stirred and after that
its sole purpose
was to continue

There was no escaping that

movement to movement
and as it moved
many things clung to it

so that it appeared
constantly different

And it never knew itself
could never know
what it once had been

5

The telling of stories
recalls the dead

Come
      they say
you are us
not what you think you are

It is *that* which makes you suffer
in the essence of your solitude

But we are all that matters
in birth in life and in death
through which you shall join us
enter our world of the lie
of the false self holding you apart

What need have you to fear
your return to us
ever vigilantly awaiting it
ever attentive to your longings

Listen to our voices
They will dispel your loneliness
Do not concern yourself
with the manner of your going
It is the return that counts

We reach you through
story
     poem
         music
            sex

From time to time
we have left our place of undying
to become you
to show you the way to us
by example
taking on your lies

We are most present
in such things as
the frail pace of the old
They are nearest to us
their tired selves falling away
like leaves
baring the branches of endurance

And children
who
        like animals
have not yet left us

All biographies are lies
all autobiographies are lies

There are only the rare moments
when self-lies are revealed

After a lifetime of search
a lone man looks out at the sea
and knows at last what he is
the rest is the waiting

The old woman at the window
stroking her cat

her familiar
quietly bides her time
unblinded by sunlight

6

When sickness came then
kindness also came

Not the rancour
that comes so often now
in these late times of tiredness
impatience
           with the steady collapse of things
rot under the peeling paint
aches in the creaking timbers
draughts through the warped doors

It wasn't the customary grapes he brought
but small sweet tomatoes
green-topped
succulent
fragrant

He knew what you liked
For this was no casual gift

It is never known at the time
that a gift such as this
unlike all others
maybe extravagant and ceremonial
will outlive the giver

A taste embedded in the palate of memory
evoking always that kindness
and a hopeless melancholy

It will die only when the body dies

7

Mother was cooking her head in the oven

It is not possible to forget such a sight

Her note said
Look after your baby sister

How not to remember such things

The body tired with sickness
crawls toward any available escape-hatch

It may be air or gas or a kicked chair

Nothing matters but leaving
Farewell Farewell my darlings
It is not that I am going to a better place
I am leaving because I cannot stay

It was never mentioned later
not even after she did die
but not of her own choosing

O never say Goodbye
but simply See you later

8

The picture on the wall Father drew
is quite professional you know

★

O tell me no more of such things

★

In his bohemian days
he learnt to paint from a master

★

O but he had no bohemian days

*He was imprisoned for 30 years
as a shop assistant
selling fine garments
to the gentry of the city*

★

He knew all the intricacies
of the combustion engine

Could dismantle the whole thing
and put it together in a day

★

O but his car was an old banger

★

He knew all the cities of the world
their museums and art galleries
and the histories of many of them
★
O but his sole journey of any length
was a trip across the Irish Sea

★

His memory was as well stocked as an encyclopaedia

★

O but after Mother died
he could disburse nothing but sadness

★

He was a happy man
intelligent and quick-witted

★

O but it all failed him in the end

SUCH AS FLICKER

I

Flicker in darkness,
stumble on pavement,
bump on cobble,
abrupt knock of head,
or oddly oriented nod,
or, then, maybe, later,
I'm sorry to have
to tell you but . . .

Map me the soul
in the brain's neurons . . .
not what moves eye flicker
or movement of limb
or even speech . . .

What year is it?
Where do you live?
When were you born?
Where are you now?
How many fingers do you see?

I don't know.

Questions relevant
only, possibly,
to fixables,
answered
so I can walk again
as I did before,
as ignorantly,
in the same
darkness.

To walk on
we may say,
ignorantly,
in the darkness,
unquestioning
as before,
sufficing with
the here-and-now
as always,
dyspeptic, euphoric,
depending on circumstance,
avoiding always.

II

I watched
the old lady.

The neighbours laid her
out on her bed
in her own room, cleansed
of excrement,
not smelling sweetly
but fragrant
in the candle's odour,
and the uncustomary silence
of the slum street.

Touch her
touch her.
She is cold
as winter stone,
and as unanswerable.

Tell me, please, tell me.

Daringly
I touched her flesh:
cardboard.

TELL ME YOUR STORY

'Tell me your story,'
said the crow to the owl.
'You who have wisdom
and know all the answers.'

And the owl just hooted,
blinked and hooted.

'Why do you sing?'
asked the crow of the blackbird.

And the blackbird alighted
on a branch and simply sang.

And so it went on:
sparrow and wagtail,
thrush and finch,
linnet and redpoll:
all were interrogated.

But all went about their business
and met the crow's questions
in their own way.

And the crow, despondent,
went back to the roadway
to scavenge
as he had always done.

THE TROUBLED SOUL

We poets in your youth begin in gladness,
But thereof come in the end despondency and madness.
                              William Wordsworth

He walked the streets of the undead.
Before his eyes drunks fell into their graves.
Merchants in pinstripe dealt in rags and bones.

Beyond the city, cemeteries dominated the landscape.
Nightingales croaked above leprous willows.
The bells of empty churches tolled sadly.

Blue shadows on limed walls stalked him.
One was his sister's, whose endearments
abated his loneliness but pained him to the quick.

Where was he going? Beyond an imposed self
no longer himself, to create a new self.
But whom and out of what to create a new self?

Delving into the depths of the dead
in vain he sought answers to his distress.
Then back to a dark sky and flashes of lightning.

In his madness
he traversed plains in search of redemption
for himself and all his kind.

Demons not angels
danced on the needle point of his mind.

THE PORT

The port gorges and disgorges
cargo
effluvial detritus
sludges downriver

Crabs cling to the granite embankment

Large grey mullets
deathly white
float against the river's debile
current

I hide on the last of the granite steps
where the river-ferries
arrive and depart
on the half-hour
carrying workmen from north & south
south & north
paying their pence

No money yet
or time
for me
to pay the ferryman

I had not yet learnt the alphabet
the church angelus my only chronometer
time time time

regina coeli
for him thou wast worthy to bear

No matter

Eyes and ears suck waves
slapping against memory

The crabs cling to the decapitated fishheads

DEAD POETS' SOCIETY

I am tired talking to myself

and those around me
involuntary eavesdroppers

They, too, are tired
listening to me
talking to myself

I should invent
a persona to talk to

lock myself away
and talk to this persona

But that too
would be
merely talking to myself
once again

So I talk to the dead
who have no choice
but to listen to me

And they answer back
as they have a right to
and it's my turn to listen

Approaching Song

dawn is about to break
the song of the blackbird
high in the silver birch
melody irritates the dark quiet
re-minding and re-minding and re-minding
over the sleeping houses
so many dawns like this like this
singing without solace
mindless morning celebrant

daybreak birdsong
tireless repetition wearies
insistent mindlessness
pains the unsleeping
high involuntary song
recalls the day
days before and days again
for the solitary
winds memory more tense more tense

Approaching White

a white pigeon flashed across the window
the summer sunlight glinted on its breast
no bird of peace this but an omen
the brief beauty of new-fallen snow
a single candle-flame extinguished
a child once held such a quick white bird
the eyes of age blink, are blind again
abrupt clack of wings and silence then
flash of bright light in a dark mind

something flashes across the eye
inciting terror
It flashes by
and is forgotten
then forgotten again
an image flashes across the eye
the solitary child
in the darkness

APPROACHING COLD

the cold of oblivion, summer is done
river turns to glinting furrow
pool becomes pit of peril
clamour of birds without shelter
white snow winds towards the door
falling flakes wide as wether's skin
raindrops broad as a shield
quick frost binds the pathways
men shudder and cry cold

homeless bird screams
in the frost-vice of winter
home warmth is not forgotten
hear the pain in the scream
there is a frozen sun in the sky
the air chills to the bone
calamitous this winter world
flight without destination
pain shrieks in the cold air

APPROACHING MOON MIND

doom approaches and the moon is cleft in two
who dares say the moon has no heart
a god measured the distance from the moon to the sun
when the clouds fly the moon travels
the moon in the water is only mind
the moon is a coin in the gutter
sister moon waxing and waning
who declares the ages of the moon
the eye of the moon at the well's end

light and dark of the moon's reflection
the eye peers into the well's end
is it the moon in the sky
or the gazer's eye
a god is the measure of distance
look into the moon's eye
and the movement of cloud
if one could defy that movement
would the heart be at rest then

APPROACHING WATER

I seek shade in the trees and the trees wither
the orange tree of your patio threw its flowers at your feet
open my gate and look into the farthest nook
seeing you the flowers of your garden wept
the day you were born all the flowers were born
the nightingales sang in the garden fountain
they have taken from me the rose that is mine
I thought I was the only one who watered your garden
the unwatered tree is dry at the roots

unreal garden of love
garden of pleasure
garden of delight
where the flowers weep silver dew
where orange blossoms scent the air
the stone toad croaks
at the nightingale's descant
'Make me some shoes with high heels'

APPROACHING LANDSCAPE

the steeples escaped bone skeletons from the churches
each word murmured was a vow and a plea
white gulls filled the lakes like ash
the sky clouded with gouged-out eyes of stars
we went on drifting with ardent brands
timeless the clocks stared
sightless eyes were blind in the bushes
into the short ban fell mortar claps of murder
underneath there dwelt despondent fear

Approaching Terminus

going nowhere it's the old story
time up and no reprieve
farewell goodbye what word matters
you saw it coming but no matter
no harder than coming but knowing
tell me there's another way
map me the soul in the brain's neurons
pattern of leaves in the wind
snow flicking its cotton-tails

Comings & Goings

1

The carved gallery
No looking back to the old land
Last night on the balcony
The rosy cheek

2

The rosy cheek
So much has already happened
When will it end
The eastward flow

3

The eastward flow
When will it end
So much has already happened
The rosy cheek

4

The rosy cheek
Spring blossom & autumn moon
It has changed
The east wind

5

The east wind
A whole river
Bright moon
The eastward flow

6

The eastward flow
Bright moon
A whole river
An east wind

7

An east wind
Still there
Jade steps
The carved gallery

8

The carved gallery
Jade steps
Still there
An east wind

9

An east wind
A while river
Bright moon
The eastward flow

10

The eastward flow
In spring
How much sorrow
The carved gallery

11

The rosy cheek
Last night on the balcony
No looking back to the old land
The carved gallery

12

The carved gallery
How much sorrow
In spring
The eastward flow

13

The eastward flow
In spring
How much sorrow
The carved gallery

14

A whole river
It has changed
How much sorrow
No looking back to the old land

15

No looking back to the old land
How much sorrow
It has changed
A whole river

16

Last night on the balcony
Spring blossom & autumn moon
In spring
Bright moon

17

Bright moon
In spring
Spring blossom & autumn moon
Last night on the balcony

BREAD OF NOSTALGIA

Joy comes in the most unexpected of moments.
It's never found when sought for earnestly
or with wild expectations
or with predatory intent.

By chance a fragrance wafts from a bakery door
and a lost world is instantly restored.

I am holding Mother's hand.
Nothing is said.

We enter the bakery
and Mother buys a loaf of oven-hot bread.
Its skin is scorched, almost black.

Still nothing is said.

This is the communion of bread
to be sliced not broken
on the raw deal of the kitchen table.

Cold butter melts like honey in the warm dough.
The scorched skin flakes on the table.

I am happy beyond time.

We still do not talk
as we sip our tea
from the chalices of our chipped cups.

Author's Note

The Dublin that is the locus of many of these poems has largely disappeared. I trust that this will make no difference to the reader, as the poems have no aspiration to be topographical or strictly descriptive.

I have decided to omit the dedications that appeared in many of these poems when they were originally printed. The persons to whom the dedications were addressed already know which poems were addressed to them and therefore such dedications are of little or no relevance to the general reader and may even be a distraction in some cases.

LaVergne, TN USA
30 September 2009
159507LV00010B/73/P

ed Poems

Also by Michael Smith:

POETRY
With the Woodnymphs
Times and Locations
Familiar Anecdotes
Stopping to Take Notes
Selected Poems
Lost Genealogies & Other Poems
Meditations on Metaphors
The Purpose of the Gift. Selected Poems

TRANSLATIONS
Pablo Neruda: *Twenty Love Poems & a Poem of Despair*
Antonio Machado: *Early Poems*
Miguel Hernández: *Unceasing Lightning*
Francisco de Quevedo: *On the Anvil*
Luis de Góngora: *Selected Shorter Poems*
Federico García Lorca: *The Tamarit Poems*
Maldon & Other Translations

César Vallejo:
> *Trilce*
> *The Complete Later Poems 1923–1938*
> *Selected Poems*
> *The Black Heralds & Other Early Poems*
> (all with Valentino Gianuzzi)

Rosalía de Castro: *Selected Poems*
Gustavo Adolfo Bécquer: *Collected Poems – Rimas* (ed. Luis Ingelmo)
Claudio Rodríguez: *Collected Poems* (with Luis Ingelmo)
Miguel Hernández: *The Prison Poems*

AS EDITOR:
James Clarence Mangan: *Selected Poems*
Irish Poetry: The Thirties Generation